# Beyond the Chandeleurs

# Beyond the Chandeleurs

*poems*

## DAVID MIDDLETON

Louisiana State University Press   *Baton Rouge*

1999

Designer: Michele Myatt Quinn
Typeface: AGaramond
Typesetter: Coghill Composition Co., Inc.
Printer and binder: Thomson-Shore, Inc.

Library of Congress Cataloging-in-Publication Data

Middleton, David, 1949–
    Beyond the chandeleurs : poems / David Middleton.
        p.   cm.
    ISBN 0-8071-2377-3 (cloth : alk. paper). — ISBN 0-8071-2377-3 (hc
: alk. paper)
    I. Title.
PS3563.I362B49   1999
811'.54—dc21                                                                99-33409
                                                                            CIP

    A number of these poems appeared—sometimes in slightly different form—in the
chapbooks *A Garland for John Finlay* (Blue Heron Press, 1990), *Louisiana Laurels* (Arts
Council of Greater Baton Rouge, 1991), *As Far as Light Remains* (Cummington Press,
1993), and *Bonfires on the Levee* (Blue Heron Press, 1996); and in the anthology *Odd
Angles of Heaven: Contemporary Poetry by People of Faith*, edited by Janet McCann and
David Craig (Harold Shaw Publishers, 1994). Also, the author wishes to thank the editors
of the following journals for publishing many of the poems herein collected: *The Angli-
can: A Journal of Anglican Identity, Anglican Theological Review, Churchwork: Episcopal
Diocese of Louisiana, Explorations, Burning Light: A Journal of Christian Literature, Hellas:
A Journal of Poetry and the Humanities, Image: A Journal of the Arts and Religion, Louisiana
English Journal, Louisiana Review, Paintbrush: A Journal of Poetry and Translation, Poiesis,
Sewanee Review, Southern Review,* and *Xavier Review.*
    Special thanks to Charles C. Clark—scholar, editor, friend.

for all who live in the given world,
especially
Andrew Lytle,
who took "the long view"
and loved the permanent things

and

in memory of
Don Stanford,
"illumined and refined"
poet, scholar, critic, mentor, friend

If a miracle could happen, every man as craftsman
would know again he has only one contemplation,
the mystery of God, made manifest in the natural order.

—Andrew Lytle, "A Myth in a Garden," 1986

✳

There is neither speech nor language;
but their voices are heard among them.

—Psalm 19:3

# CONTENTS

# Beyond the Chandeleurs

# Louisiana Passage: The Whippoorwill

*for Jack Wise*

A night or two in April, then no more
They call in latest twilight from the skies,
Migrants who fly between the stars and foam
Now come to this hard ground where dark abides.
And when the moon illumines each chill bloom
Of dandelion and violet and flag
Still trembling in a latent winter gloom,
The birds sing their own name so clean and clear—
*Whip-poor-will, whip-poor-will, whip-poor-will*—then
Swooping to scoop up insects on the wing,
Mayflies and ladybugs in those wide mouths,
They feed and fly away to nesting-grounds
Remote from those the Caddo once had known
Deep in the virgin stands of silent pine.

And yet in gold October they return
Ghostly over the uplands' folded wolds,
Riding the ancient flyway as they climb
Into a dawn where centuries ago
Their ancestors had crossed without a cry
Green kingdoms of the oak and tupelo
Unbroken from the Ozarks to the coast.
And pausing there upon the last chenier,
Made voiceless as they gaze beyond the Gulf
Toward some most catholic South their flight implies,
They listen with intent for one who calls
Each creature in the language of its name,
And when they hear they pass through silent skies
Toward Adam and the earthly paradise.

# The Sunday School Lesson

north Louisiana


The room was full of thirteen-year-old boys
Unhappily constrained by polished shoes,
Bow ties, oiled hair, orders against all noise,
And one eternal hour of Good News.

I joined the class each summer in July
When visiting my kin in that small town,
Lazing away the weeks till by and by
The signs of autumn brought my parents down.

Distracted like the rest, I, too, was bored
Though not a friend who shared the cycling year's
High rites of church, school, fair, and sports that stored
A common mind with common loves and fears.

Long-legged and ungainly in my chair,
I'd lean on the shoved-up window while the fan
Would spin a weightless haze of heated air
Around the sullen room as class began.

Jack Hopkins was our teacher though I doubt
He ever saw himself as any more
Than someone who could see an hour out
With tall tales of his catch the night before.

I'd watch his bulbous nose and long-drawn face
Both reddened in a steady heart's decline
As once more he would tell, with skill and grace,
Of nine-pound bass caught on a two-pound line.

One day, though, he seemed different, hardly there,
Gazing over the graves with restless eyes,

Searching for something distant and yet near,
Unfixable in cloudless summer skies.

At last, he slowly read, then half-recited
In a strong drawl which measured out King James,
Those passages in Matthew where affrighted
Disciples cried to Jesus as He came

Walking across night's foam upon the water
To grasp weakening Peter who'd looked down,
Distracted by the winds that made him totter,
Now mastered by the fear that he would drown.

Fumbling with his glasses, Mr. Jack then tried
With chuckles and an animated glance
Around a room from which all sound had died
To end the solemn calm and his own trance.

Those verses always moved him, he confessed,
Because of that strange evening on the lake
When a sudden storm caught him and he pressed
Against its wind to reach a cypress brake.

Perhaps it was the play of dark and light
Or just his tiredness vivified with fear,
And yet he swore that at the torrent's height
He saw the Christ by lightning drawing near.

With that, the lesson ended and the class
Rose awkwardly one by one and left the room
Embarrassed, even scared to have to pass
This man who'd gazed beyond the body's doom.

And though time brought him soon to what he saw,
It took me over thirty years to know
How soul's redeemed by wonder, lost in awe
Before those depths through which I, too, must go

With doubt and faith like Peter on the sea
Sinking in fear and chaos of the foam
Yet looking up toward one who has to be
There before the winds to take us home.

# Toward North Louisiana

*for the Literary Forum of Bastrop, Louisiana*


Driving along the bayou through Lafourche
Then up the River Road past Baton Rouge,
Going to read my poetry once more
In those small north Louisiana towns
So like the one in which this life began
Some thirty years ago—my Eden-place,
Saline—addressing those arch arbiters
Of taste, the women's reading clubs, all named
The Literary Circle, Friends of Books,
The Sunday Afternoon Association
Or some such like, so seldom deeply moved
By those whose books their members often scorn
As merely modern, rootless, crude, untrue:
I take the interstate outside of Bunkie
Under an unrelenting puritan sun—
Now westering, remote, yet still intense—
Leaving behind the boggy coastal arpents
Gone back to goldenrod and indigo
For those plain farms of pole beans, squash, and corn
Beside whose lonely houses lately placed
Satellite dishes whiten toward Orion.

I make good time and so in time I turn
Onto a slower road the state maintains
And then a sand-and-gravel parish lane
To see the ghostly groves of old pecans
Grown on the soul's home ground. And there
Where fall's gold twilight holds them in one fire
Of sun and moon and stars, the holy boles
Whose limbs hang thick with clustered hulls take flame
Above an earth the matted shadows claim.
I stop and walk among them for a spell—
The past brought back by elegiac mind—

Trespassing there as here because compelled
By love toward sacred acres undisplaced,
Seedbeds of the weathered essences we sense
When a great horned owl, its feathers widely spread,
Dropping in quiet through curled and bitter leaves
Claws the stunned mouse, then quickly reascends
Gliding under the moon to take its prey
Into the blue seclusion of the trees.

Such literal appearances remain
Hard verses in the Bible of the things,
Jehovah's old and fatal delegations
Interspersed among those palmy psalms
Whose gladder affirmations we would sing,
Whispers risen from red clay to the bluffs
Where dogwood bracts grow rusty in the sun,
Interpretable words ever kept in trust
Both spoken of and from this native place
Coming to us whose tongues become their own.

So when I'm called to read to seasoned souls
For whom the Word still echoes in the hills
They hear no single voice or slanted line,
But if we all are stewards of the gifts
We join as one in praising what is made—
Anthems of river sand and hymns of limbs
Sagging with apples, blazoning roulades
Of redbirds blessed with Pentecostal song—
And even in those oaks whose heavy arms,
Glutted with nuts, owls grip with dripping claws
We hear not just the dreaded designata,
The clammy lamentations of the blood,
But fluent *whoos* proclaiming Adam's names
Here in the bleaker reaches of the north
Whose winters grace the pines with riming glaze.

# Azaleas in Epiphany

*for Father Robert Cooper*

Delicate hot-pink bloom,
The first chill hint of spring,
Aflame outside my room,
What message do you bring?

Some think you self-sufficient,
Spontaneously there,
Mute matter's co-efficient,
Unfolding unaware.

But I can only deem
As holy petioles
And pedicels that teem,
Leaf-tongues and petal-scrolls.

Thus taken, in their stations,
All things are angels sent
Blazing into creation,
The Word's embodiment.

# FOR AN ARTIST WITH PARKINSON'S

*in memory of my father, David V. Middleton, Jr.*
*(1922–1996)*


So still beside the window in a chair
Whose wheels you cannot move and barely clutch,
You scan with eyes harsh medicine has blurred
A winter world once rendered by your touch.
Black seed-pods and a last few orange leaves
Crackling in dwarf crape myrtles, stark pecans
Mistletoed and bared of leaf and nut, grackles
Cracking berries in the frosted holly groves—
All these you stained in ink, the pot's baked glaze,
Or brought alive in oils—those earthen shades
Made from the very things whose shapes they made.

When you were in your prime I was a child
Held tight in the softened muscles of your hug
Riding on your shoulders while the spring
Grew wild with buttercups and ladybugs.
On summer days, heat pouring from above
Beat strong on your hard arm that hammered down
Long boards to roof a workshop where you wrought—
Absorbed in the timeless habitude of craft—
God's objects set aflame with human love.
And though your gift was modest, still in kind
You knew the joy of Buonarroti's mind.

One day in fall now forty years ago
You took me to a sloping melon field
That crested in an oak whose thickest limb
I straddled as you sketched me from below.
Evasive of your gaze grown so intense
I stared down at the dried and shriveled vines,
Dreaming of greenest rinds in late July
And heard in the still green needles of the pine

Faint windblown strains refining to a quiet
In which a newborn gift delayed by grace
First stirred as you shaded-in my gazing face.

Now you are old and ill beyond all art
Yet just as when you sketched me on the day
My head of curls was wreathed in curling leaves
And I was drawn and chosen we still serve
The Giver of our gifts: for when I draft
Quiet poems upon this table whose thick top,
Split with hard use, you covered up at last
With plastic sheets held taut by roofing nails
My pen moves where you painted, stained, and glazed
Giving for years to beauty and the muse
Those hands a child had thought would never fail.

# A QUIET REPLY

*for my mother, Anna Sudduth Middleton,*
*who became a housewife and mother in the 1940s*
*in north Louisiana*

The house is silent now, yet through the rooms
Once filled with laughter, music, talk, and tears
I hear the sounds of children who will play
As long as love still draws their spirits near.
And there beside a window what remains
Of my good husband stares across the yard
At that locked greenhouse he cannot recall
Ever having built or even seen before.
His pension, savings, what the children send
Will do until he dies and I move in
With one of them to live in that last room
With pictures and the pictures in my mind.
A housewife and a mother who performed
The common sacraments of daily life
On stove and tabletop and ironing board,
I thought my work a calling, nothing less.
My sons' wives seem to think me incomplete
Yet there they are, outraged by their own tears
When toddlers left at day-care cling and scream
Torn from their mothers' arms before the dawn
And not picked up till dusk by those who gave
Their best at work and now crave rest alone.
I hold my tongue and let its quiet reply
Be answer to their barely hidden guilt
That would in me have cried out from the heart
Where deepest things can never be denied.
But still I pause and try to understand
The kind of lives they say they have to live
And wonder whether I am one of those
Whose bent was taken late from ancient ways
Now passing with the world I used to know.

And yet I still remember and remain
In that sweet peace I entered long ago
Trusting in those old customs love sustains
By sacrifice till truth is realized.
Our wedding night on which we gave ourselves
As virgins to the ways of man and wife,
Those early months before the children came,
That small garage apartment where we lived
On what a navy seaman was allowed,
Then parenthood that bonded us in joy
And duty to the family and to God—
Such blessings were the laws that set me free
Through all those years the children were at home—
Nursing them with milk from my own heavy breasts,
Coming to calm their night fears with a hug,
Watching them sleep and wake, helping them walk,
Reading them Bible stories, Mother Goose,
Teaching them colors, numbers, shapes, and words,
And showing them the games I used to play,
Ring-around-the-roses, hopscotch, hide-and-seek.
And for my love of them, my husband, too,
I made a home for us as best I could
And welcomed every task I had to do,
Washing the breakfast dishes, folding clothes,
Cleaning the house or going to the store,
Gardening and sewing, working at church,
Absorbed in the sacred making of the day.
Thanksgiving, Christmas, Easter, summertime,
The births and birthdays, marriages and deaths—
These were the greater and the lesser feasts
That filled life's calendar with poignancies.

The children now of course are grown and gone,
My husband only waiting, tired of life,
My days with him but disciplined routines
Of food and drugs, of silences and naps,
Then bed in which each struggling breath sustains
A body all but ready for its death.

I know he soon will pass away and I
Will leave this house in which for fifty years
We found our place within a settled world
Where God permits us all to apprehend
The nature of creation and its end.
And what will I remember when I go
To live my final years in that last room
One of my children must prepare for me?
The night I showed my husband our firstborn
Was kicking in the womb I made him press,
The first warm cup of tea those autumn dawns
I relished in the coolness on the porch
Before my family woke, or that quiet day
I told my youngest child about the time
The sun stood still for Joshua while outside
That very sun at noon shone down again
On irises that seemed to bloom and bloom
Forever in those lingering full beams
Until our eyes grew bright with selfless love.
Such moments stay alive within my heart
And in this private journal where for years
I've filled so many pages, not with rage,
But love preserved in memory's glad tears.

# ANCIEN RÉGIME

South Lafourche

*for John Doucet*

The night spreads out along its native plain
Whose lights still shine as they have always shone
Inside the burning manors that remain
So long as souls respond with love alone

As they do here where salty floods subside
Before the old plantations' lower fields
And bulging trucks rumble through Christmastide
Strewing tall stalks of cane from record yields.

Stray offerings made to harvest gods that die,
The stalks are crushed to splinters under cars
While overhead where heaven binds the sky
The Dippers pour forth darkness from their stars.

And though we have been told the time has come
To know the earth unhallowed, merely here,
It is a creed too bleak for Christendom
In which a child drew kings and shepherds near:

And so we hold these fields of sweetest dust
Like Mary, who submitted to the Lord,
The Father and the Son, in utmost trust,
Freely compelled by all her soul adored

For then alone do constellations sing
Of God's collations underneath the moon,
A primal rhyme of image, thought, and thing
Still moving to an unprecluded noon.

# Ex Nihilo

He left the cave, drawn by a winter moon
That bared the only world its light could find,
An unimagined land of gradeless shades
Transfigured in a random pantomime
Of some black pastoral that had to be.
On distant holy hills the shadow-swains
Piping the wordless dirges of the res
Ravished his heart until its maiden cries,
Melodic in the somber minor keys,
Soared toward untransposable refrains.
A frosty spirit chastened by its breath,
He burned in cold remoteness as the stars
Blazing against the night they hate and crave
Soon twinkled out and fell so far away
They reached a place no place could realize.
Fearful of desire, the given, happenstance,
He sifted finest particles of dark
Dug from the moonlit claypools of the cave,
Grinding the dust of nothing to create
The bleak Matter of Matter—his romance.

✳

After the vows, the tossed bouquet, champagne,
He sought in the moaning flesh his tongue aroused
Articulate embodiment, a vital
Dialogue with the substance of his craft.
Yet, in the rhythmed heaves of breath and sex,
He sensed only a rude, mocking, inadept
Variation on his own unmetrical text.
Objectified and used, thus truly loved

As cold young poets love, when words failed
She left those rooms where he stayed on alone
That rich and bitter spring, seeing no one,
Losing himself in notebooks, cheap red wine,
Lonely acts of lust, and drunken sleep.
To free himself from chaos and despair
He wrote Shelleyan sonnets to the moon,
Courting the muse with floral catalogues,
Bright likenesses all heightened from the life,
Bouquets of white narcissi, passionflowers,
Names of the imaged things once bred from love,
Gifts of the one who comes but never weds.

＊

Midsummer's green domain grown stark and hard,
The modulated planes of dark and light—
Split in the cryptic prism of his verse—
Were strained through screens of Christendom and Greece.
Yet drenched in the viscid tissues of the brain
His mind became its own dread messenger
Telling not of a god whose silence
Lets us speak but a mumbling demiurge.
Meanwhile, in time, a needlewoman came
Who only asked to love him as he was.
At night, when he had suffered long enough
Drafting a verse to gloss the utmost crux,
She made him close his book of Genesis
Then took him deep inside her till they cried,
Dependent creatures helpless in their joy,
Sharing to the full the things they fully craved,
The gifts of love and personhood and sex,
Content with their set portion of the good.
Thereafter, when they wove their words and threads
They were each other's muse and truly wed.

＊

He waited for the mystery to fade
As Wordsworth said it would, yet on the Gulf—
Their voices sweetening deep into the fall—
The mockingbirds had never ceased to sing.
Late summer had alerted him: cool pre-dawns,
The paling light of shortened afternoons,
And evenings when the crickets' scattered cries
Proclaim desire itself desires an end.
Somehow, within, the old and simple wonder
Had survived, and, by its vital power,
He strove to learn the native tongue of God,
Those seminal declensions of the res,
Thing-words to which our word-things correspond.
Sometimes his daughter sought her father-god
To sing away night's goblins, ghosts, and elves,
Though like a greater maker's, it may be,
His lyrics seemed to blossom from the dark
Like autumn's Indian pipes, those nodding white
And solitary blooms, erect in fruit,
That blackened when he plucked them from the ground.

\*

And yet, at last, nurtured by faith and grace,
He came to understand and then rejoice
That darkness could not be without the light,
Each defining each as twin contingencies
Divided from the undivided One.
The countless stars, all counted, named, and known,
Migrations of the geese and galaxies
Out of the nesting-grounds of ice and fire,
Physics-in-metaphysics—the blooming root!—
Fruitions and transcendences of the fall,
All types and antitypes in the metaphors'
Confluencies of spirit, heart, and mind:
Such elements make up the measured text
Satan would break apart, opening the forms.
And so from the winter heavens it appears

That all things here are never merely here
But called and spoken into place by God
Who whispers out of the deep, His *privité*,
Sweet nothings that persuade us as we praise
Old Arcadies of darkness and the stars.

# In Acadie

A gibbous moon made full this autumn night
Shines down through chilling windows to a bed
Where lost within its pale archaic light
We only know what silent tongues have said.

No novices too eager to possess
Phantasms who elude their rude desire,
We wait till blood grown flush with each caress
Is slowly roused to climax in the fire.

Your hair's soft strands falling across my chest
As you ride me high in rhythms willed and random,
My warm lips sucking gently on your breasts,
My firm control sustaining your abandon—

This is the sweet confessional of flesh
Where words both raw and tender will be said
Which, when we wake to innocence afresh,
Remain behind in silence and the bed.

And though in darkened windows darker skies
Proclaim the stark contingency of light
In stars that burn and die in bright reprise
Of some prime cause which moved against the night,

Here in a world reproved by constant love,
In bodies we possess but for a time,
Live wedded souls made one by One above
Who came to earth that love might be sublime.

# THE HERON AT THE WEIR

on Bayou Lafourche,
between Canal and Jackson Street,
Thibodaux, Louisiana

*for Don Stanford (1913–1998)*

So still amid the foam that plays
About his legs the heron stays
Atop a rock below the weir
That brings the silver minnows near.

He knows that what the weir provides
The darkly flowing bayou hides
Until the spray breaks at his feet
And offers up bright fish to eat.

His gaze seems fixed and icon-like
Till beak and eye by instinct strike
Taking a prey that never heeds
The reedy legs it sees as reeds.

And there amid the things that change
The heron stays so still and strange
Within a quiet he all but hears,
An earthly music of the spheres.

# Stars at Noon

*for Father George Walker, rector,*
*St. John's Episcopal Church,*
*Thibodaux, Louisiana*

Throughout the dawn they vanish one by one,
Those stars that still proclaim the ancient night,
Screened off by blinding rays of our own sun
Which brings the day's blue dome of air and light.

And in that dome the mind has come to know
Each creature made and stationed in its place
By Him who left us shepherds long ago
Of all His meadowlands of time and space.

Magnolias holding huge white blooming moons,
Pelicans scooping minnows from the tides,
Sunflowers climbing high in cloudless noons
Or bowing while the twilight still abides:

Such palpable abstractions as they fare—
The gleaming things, the brazen shapes ablaze—
Grow holy and beholden unaware
Of those galactic pastures where they graze.

And when, beyond the darkness and the stars—
Those primal givens riven from the One—
We find the great foundation nothing mars
In that First Cause who willed each brilliant sun

Then deep within the heavens' stellar wells
We sense a love whose overflowing glow
Still claims us when we gaze toward where it dwells
And matter seems no longer all we know

Just as the stars at noon are ever there,
Remembered and expected, though unseen,
Flaring against the darkness they declare
As like themselves, a part of what they mean.

# Night Fears: A Lullaby

*for my daughter, Anna, at two*

Shaken from a dream
Of dark and starry lands
I waken to your scream
And feel the tiny hand
By which you made your way
Along the shadowed hall
Searching for the day
With teddy bear and doll.
And as you hug so tight
This father whom you love
I know you fear the night
Within us and above.

And so I come to place
Beside your rumpled bed
A night light with the face
Of some bright star that sheds
Its glowing painted smile
On gloomy walls and shelves
To keep you safe awhile
From bogies, ghosts, and elves.
All tucked in now between
The new bed's guard-rail bars
You sleep again and dream
Of fathers and the stars.

Then kissing you good night
I sit in dark alone
And wonder if you might
Recall when I am gone
And it is you instead
Whose own night-frightened child
Stands crying by your bed

With eyes so wide and wild
How you too sobbed in fright
For one no longer here
Who brought a little light
And held you warm and near.

For where no teddy bear,
No talisman of stone,
Or faintest breath of air
Can go we go alone
Far down that blackest hall
Of echoes dead and hollow
Through which no toddler's calls
Or footsteps can follow.
Yet even in that place
A Father from afar
Bestows His love and grace,
The night lights of the stars.

# WALKING THE ROOTS

*to Anna*

Your once uncertain toddling being strengthened
Into the steady rhythm of a walk,
Your seed-words sprouting out in sentences,
In your own early spring you gazed on spring
And knew the word-things God, in saying, made.
Purple maple leaves as tender as your hand,
Green stalks of pussy willow tall as you,
Tasseling oaks and rampant dandelions—
Such things, in the beginning you construed
From taintless names, the grammar of creation,
And there you found, in soundings of the One,
Identity, the true similitude.

Then clambering onto my shoulders you would sing
Into the wordless voicings of the wind,
And when I heard the blending, like a child
I felt my heart beat fast with love again.
You pointed everywhere at everything
Demanding names—"What's *that?*"—then tried them out
On cardinals and robins, dragonflies,
Periwinkles, marigolds and slugs,
But most on slinky caterpillars creeping
In shadowed grass, massing on the great pecan
To climb and spin cocoons that butterflies
Might lose themselves in blossom-scent and light.

And swinging you up there overhead and down,
I showed you how to step from root to root,
Each one sinking deep in mind and ground.
Your stiff left arm bracing against rough bark,
You giggled gingerly—caught off guard
By anthills, thorny bramble, unraked leaves,
And quick green lizards—yet made it back around

To where we'd packed and smoothed the hauled-in dirt.
"Write ANNA!" you cried, and so, with a stick,
I wrote the stick-like letters in the dust
That held you as you watched your symboled self
Emerge from earth and essence as it must.

And asking those old questions born of wonder—
"What is night?" "Where do the stars come from?"
"What's behind the sky?" "Why is the moon the moon?"—
You started to probe the surfaces of things.
And though you walked on roots clutched at some black depth
By matter's shapeless hell—you looked beyond
Topmost boughs leafing out toward heaven and saw
Bright clouds condensing under the aether-fields
Marking as home this designated place
Prepared by One who speaks unceasingly
Through every plant and animal and star
And every child who names the things that are.

# EMBERTIDE IN ADVENT

*for J. R. W.*

They waited beneath the cold December snows,
Late flowers of the fall, the folded rose,
The angels'-trumpet crumpled in the mold,
Daisies of Michaelmas, the hidden lily curled
In dust of goldenrod and marigold,
Old matter's liturgy, a pregnant world
Out of whose star-of-Bethlehem arose
A Roman hyacinth, sweet-olive of the snows.

# DINNER ON THE GROUND

When Moses sent them to explore Canaan, he said,
"Go up . . . into the hill country. See what the land is like."
—Numbers 13:17

*Caroll Eubanks (1919–1997), i.m.*


You drove us there at twilight last July
Up roads that ran through memory's summer realm
Leading into a deep primeval green
Where memory itself is overwhelmed.
Then just one slope below the weathered crest
We paused where a sleeping meadow made its bed
Over the Old Spring Church's flowering graves
Whose headstones nod forever toward the dead.
And there a sign's blunt letters raised in bronze
Before a house of God no souls possess
Told stories of a congregation's fate,
"Part of our state's rich history" . . . nothing more . . .
This church whose firm believers lie so still
Below the untilled soil their plows once turned
Like pages of a faith's inerrant text.

The slabs preserved brief annals of their lives,
A birth and death date, Bible verse or rhyme
For Enloe, Weaver, Evans, Hopkins, Toms,
Descended souls whose own descendants filled
A vanished world in which you had been born
Near eighty years ago in these same hills.
You called the common things by proper names—
Hardscrabble Point, Owl's Hollow, Choctaw Creek—
And going on for hours down bramble-paths
Would seek out churchless graveyards long reclaimed
By overgrowth, then prop up marking-stones
On which you read a culture's epitaph.
And while the twilight shaded into night

Whose stars provoke the dark with spoken light
You begged us just to listen for a spell
As winds blew through the cedars in reprise
Of all you now felt so compelled to tell.

Your heart gave up its deep most urgent words
And as we looked around we almost saw
Emerging from the greenwood's waking glades
Some Sabbath dawn a hundred years ago
On foot, horse, mule, or clackety wagon-seat
Folk set to spend their day of rest with God,
The gaunt tall men in black, the women prim
Yet comely in their hand-sewn Sunday clothes—
The clinging blooms of gingham, calico—
And children running in homespun till all hushed
And waiting on the cushionless straightback pews.

Beyond those souls, the Table of the Lord,
White pine stained dark as though with Christ's own blood,
Above which rose a pulpit where the sun
Reached down until a single finger-beam
Fell on the burning words the pastor read
With Jacobean accents clearly heard
In Holy Writ and backwoods southern speech.
He preached to them of Canaan and the spies
Who, in the Valley of Clusters, gathered up
From midnight groves Jehovah's starlight marked
The scattered pomegranates, grapes, and figs,
Bringing them back to Moses as a sign
His fathers' earth still held its Hebrew seed.

And when the sermon finished with a prayer,
The yeomen closed their eyes and saw their farms
Hard wrested from the wilderness—rugged slopes
Well-watered by the salt of sweat and tears
That raised up from a thin resistant soil
Spring shallots and the summer butter beans
And corn to feed the beasts that fed their flesh

After the fall's dark harvest of the blood.
And with their longings now made manifest
In tales of turning home toward Eden's fields
An older hunger drew them from the cross
Toward rows of tables laden in the pines
With floured chicken fried up to a crisp,
Deep bowls of steaming okra, squash, and greens,
Potatoes with their fluffy butter-wells,
And pots of bubbling salt-pork seasoned peas.

Then through the long slow-moving afternoon
On bedspreads dyed with native muscadine
Stern elders breathed the scented woodland air
Till drowsy, dozing, they gave in to sleep,
Dreaming a dream more ancient than their faith,
Inhalers of the fragrant pagan day.
Meanwhile late mating cries of mockingbirds
Would draw stray couples down old hunting trails
In silence to the virgin kissing-trees,
And there, while fingers played with ribbon ends,
Young Southern Baptist tongues found maiden mouths
So open to the firm wet searching tips
That passion drove off guilt, their chaperone,
Till blushing and reluctant they returned
To hear an evening message, then depart.

The preacher with his Bible stood alone
Beside the spring that gave the church its name,
Declaring how God made the dark and light,
The waters of the heavens and the stars,
While overhead the congregated fires
Of southern constellations held their course
Flaring out of the Lord's imperative,
Spinning the endless sentence of His will.

And so with God's two books become as one—
Pages of Genesis blazoned in the sky—
The service closed and all the farmers turned

By foot, horse, mule, and wagon toward the roads
Laid over trails first cut by buffalo
Grazing these hills twelve thousand years ago.
And as they neared their lonely homes they saw
Against the primal outline of the corn
A hay-stuffed scarecrow crucified in light
Descended from a distant quarter-moon,
His painted face so bright and unaware,
His voice a wind that rises in the maize,
Old ragged Adam working all his days
There in the very place where Michael's blade
To keep God's holy ground from mortal eyes
Swung blazing from the gates of paradise.

## OF LUNAR HISTORY

Born of the cataclysms of the core
Or captured by a weighty sway of air,
The moon stared down on earth's erupted shores,
Unnamed, unapprehended, unaware.

Then marking time so time might come to be,
Its changing light awoke inchoate mind
Which gathered from the dusty lunar seas
The Huntress and the Witch and Pluto's Bride.

And in those days when time grew great with child
Through Mary's blood whose cycles mimed its course
The moon shone on the stable and the hill
Made bright with light drawn down toward light's own source.

Yet no less bright and fair through starkest nights
It glared on Nagasaki's glowing tomb
And on those souls that suffered holocaust
In showers and the ovens and the womb.

No wonder then when in that dust and stone
Where astronauts plant flags and breathe earth's air
We see a face whose gaze contains our own
Transfixed by history's brooding lunar stare.

# FROM THE JOURNAL OF BRANWELL BRONTË

## the Black Bull Inn, Haworth, January, 1848

In this dark place where visions fail
Between black pints of Yorkshire ale
While hard against shut tavern doors
Snow blows from godforsaken moors

I think of when our father came
With soldier-toys we made a game
And then a world for which I grieve,
Play's Eden place I'll never leave.

Now Charlotte, Emily, and Anne
Write secretly apart and plan
To make the sprites of fairy tales
Gruff Yorkshiremen in Yorkshire dales.

But nothing of their novel art
Can capture Glasstown or a heart
That only some most potent brew
Or drugs console now play is through.

And though my life has been a waste
By pain, disease, and failure graced,
That life seems richer than the prose
Ambitious sisters still compose.

Yet if at last they earn their fame
Biographers will learn the name
Of one who roamed on darker moors
Than those outside the Black Bull's doors.

# The Enclosed Order

His parchment legal sheets,
A flare-tip pen his brush,
On brief internal retreats
He finds within the rush
Of ringing hours that pass
In conference and class
Eternity-in-time,
The closure of a rhyme.

Those public places sought
Across the altar rail
Or lectern where he taught
Grow private as they fail
The herbalist of words
Who knows his verse engirds
The ground he has to fill
With garlic, hyssop, dill.

Devoted to the names
Of those who kept the Word—
Tyndale, Cranmer, James—
(Grave cadences unheard)
He serves the old estate:
Incising fine and late
By Ptolemaic globe
The copper scrolls of Job.

# Along the Banks of Pischon

A river flowed out of Eden . . .
—Genesis 2:10


We saw it first and only when we raised
Eyes dazed by the primal blinding of its sheen
Flowing cold and golden as it blazed
Along the flawless fault of its ravine.

Then come from the living waters vivified
We lay on tangled banks of marigold
Sighing in scented winds that now replied
With all the holy silence had foretold.

The pomegranate, apricot, and palm
Heavy with fruit that hung forever there
Ripened in time while deep in timeless calm
The healing leaves dripped balm in balmy air.

Then one still summer noon the sun would come
To lave with light the river's cloven flow
Till shades of onyx-stone and bdellium
Shone in the golden bed that glowed below.

And there we swam within the current's surge
Then drifted as it thrilled us with our fear
Of being drowned where dark and light converge
Or so we sang as Noah's clouds drew near.

So, too, in these drained fields we find no rest
Scything the grain or pruning back the vine
While loam crumbles and foams on the river's crest
Yet still we long to taste the bread and wine

For Pischon flows from Eden like a fountain
Washing the Dead Sea clean of all its salt

Then turning round beside God's Holy Mountain
Goes flowing back again along a fault

To paradise where Adam named each thing
Under the twining boughs on either shore
Whose leaf and fruit and bloom together cling
Upon the Tree of Life forevermore.

# Junior Warden

In an Episcopal church, "the junior warden is responsible
for the maintenance of buildings and grounds."
—*A New Dictionary for Episcopalians* (1985)

*for Millicent*

My charge might seem to be the lesser thing
Like Martha's sweat to Mary's scented hair
For neither grounds nor buildings make a church
But people—as repeatedly we're told
By those whose faith may nonetheless increase
When graves are graced by lilies and the palm
And stained-glass angels fill with Easter light
That thrills me like a love-hug at the Peace.

I'm God's odd-jobber of the common task—
Blocked drains, frayed wiring, beetle-eaten trees,
The playground's rusted slides and glider-pipes,
Leached water in the floorboards, belfry bats,
And termite-rafters cracking wild in storms
That drench our sanctuary's fresco-dome
Till stars drip down behind the altar rail
On church mice munching dry unleavened crumbs.

Workdays, it seems, the parish is my own,
The priest and people mostly self-excused,
Yet those few hearty souls who come at dawn
To pull up poison ivy from the shrubs,
Scrub lichen off the sunlight whitened tombs
And paint the children's swings bright red and blue
Bond deeply in exhaustion's sweet release,
Our bodies' salt their shared mortality.

And though I still find idols in the minds
Of some who pine for worn-out things and ways—

Male vestries, deacons, priests, and fusty rites,
A church turned inward, dreaming of its past
And all those golden shields of Solomon—
I know my womanhood's essential good
In every Adam's longing for his Eve
And in each child their soulful loving brings.

So, too, at parish dinners and the Mass
In due and just proportions we receive
A foretaste of the Lamb's great wedding feast
And almost glimpse the New Jerusalem
In heaven's grounds and buildings raised by love,
God's temple of the body and the stars
Where Jesus washed the dust from Peter's feet
And made mere bread and wine His flesh and blood.

# The Deep South, the 1840s

## 1 *Frost in August*

Humid light tinges the late predawn
In black skies faintly fading deep slate blue.
Stars glint in iron heavens soon withdrawn
Beyond a pastel azure's placid hue.
Smooth limbs of the bloomed mimosas barely sway
Against the prior stillness they declare.
Short nights stay far too warm to take away
Heat poured from the brightest heights of midday air.
Along a stream the dark's departing moon
Casts down into the grass that now grows slow
Pale beams that seem more lucid than the noon
In reaching through the shades toward things below.
Mature black crickets, rubbing wing on wing,
Detect the slightest cooling in the breeze.
Later, mated females filled by what they sing
Will lay thick globs of eggs before the freeze.

## 2 *Song of the Stunted Oak*

Born of a seed that fell
Into the dark I dwell
Under an ancient spell
Here where I grew.

All through the spring I urge
Summer's green leaves to emerge
Yet the first cricket's dirge
Calls me to you.

Stunted and young I rot
Into my birthing spot,
Mother, your womb my lot,
Hail and adieu.

# THE WARGAMER

Bending the mapboard back
Unfolding Waterloo,
His fingers sift the stack
Of counters pink and blue
Into opposing groups
Of abstract cardboard troops.

Each corps, each division,
As the rules plainly state,
Must with great precision
Be placed to emulate
A history without gore,
Art of the art of war.

Wholly absorbed in play,
Indifferent to the end,
A master either way
To attack or to defend,
He doesn't have to care,
Playing solitaire.

At Quatre Bras to start
Ney battles on the heights,
Dice and the combat chart
Decide the bloodless fights
In cipher-sayings grim:
"A-back-2." "D-elim."

The dead pile grows all day,
A pink hill flecked with blue,
As Wellington gives way
And the Old Guard crashes through
Leaving the board to win
Deep in the dark Ardennes.

And so the gamer's drained
By carnage on the hexes
Where fantasy is pained
By nothing stark that vexes,
No bloated human meat,
Historical defeat.

# THE NEW WORLD

Before they saw the shore
They smelled the sweetened trees
At fifty miles or more,
Cold England's pilgrim poor,
The lion's spoor, the lees.
The strange land held its course:
They drifted toward the source.
Then, by the scrolling roar's
Blank histories of the sea,
An old hint sent before
Out of a great cat's gore,
Wild swarms of scented bees
Filled honeycombs to please
All who would ask no more.

# THE YEOMAN FARMERS:
## NORTH LOUISIANA, 1840–1914

*for the Agrarians*


We left the Carolinas in our prime
Exhausted by those bleak depleted fields
And like our fathers sought a virgin earth
Not on the eastern coastland with its waves
That brought us here from Europe's colder shores
But to the west far inland till we came
Beyond the Rio Flores to a place
Of buckled wolds uprisen from a sea
Whose salt and sand still glint in sandy hills
And saline springs that bubble from the domes.
We stopped somewhere beyond the Ouachita
In wilderness that struck bewildered eyes
As Adam's land unplowed six thousand years,
And there we swore to stay and break the soil
That we might eat its fruit as God's own words
And be at once the thing we taste and say,
Old cloven roots abloom in man and earth.

To all we saw we gave those common names
That brought the sheer appearances so near
In iron-capped hills braced against Arctic winds
Or bottomlands weighed down with graded clays,
And there in time the trees of Eden rose—
Red oak and blackjack oak, loblolly pine,
And spread along the green primeval streams
Or raft lakes rising and falling with the Red
The dogwood, hawthorn, cypress, water-elm,
Overcup oak, and willows near the bogs
Clotted with bloodroot, aster, goldenrod.
These things declared the seasons in their prime
And in their rugged coverture secured
That ground from which in our own tongue there came

Strains of an ancient anthem of the land,
A floral oratorio proclaimed
By plighted light so holy to behold:
The twayblade and the nodding indigo,
White mayhaws slashing wild through dandelions,
The early buttercups and lyre-leaved sage
Turning the springtime pastures pink and blue,
And resurrection ferns that feather the oaks
With leaves made green again in each new rain.

Such wonders trembled near us in a wind
Articulate with speeches of the trees,
And when we read the Bible and we gazed
From Holy Writ to this unbroken ground
We sometimes saw the olives of Carmel,
Philistia's headed barley, glinting grapes
Grown ripe across the bright Judean hills,
Or clustered pulpy dates of Jericho,
And as we gazed we tasted in a daze
A honeyed milk drawn sweet from salty springs.
But this at best was Eden unreclaimed,
Not paradise but forest where we shaped
By work that would have strained bent Adam's back
Each garden, orchard, pasture, pen, and field
Out of an earth no plow had ever turned.
And there the oxen dragged sharp coulter-blades
Through loam from which our seed-corn sprouted high,
Those tall green stalks long summers filled with ears
That dried in barns where like a harvest god
The welcome kingsnake slithered in the cribs.

The garden in its seasons gave and gave—
Spring's early peas and onions, summer beans,
Then mustard greens and collards through the fall
While orchards swelled the bins with ready fruits,
The apple, peach, persimmon, fig, and pear—
Riches that came alone from constant toil
In spite of storm and drought and pestilence,

Crops rotting in the shallow lakes of rain,
Then shriveled in the cracked and baking earth
Or feasted on by beetles, worms, and birds
And by disease for which we had no name.
Those years of mere subsistence fixed our wills
And we survived, thriving in privation,
Freeholders of the soul's created ground,
No longer pioneers who barely lived
Hardscrabbling day by day to eat and be
But yeomen so possessed by what we owned
The rhythms of the seasons made us sing
Plain verses turned in earth and heart and mind.
And from such work recalled in latest dusk,
The furrowed fields agleam with sweat and dew,
We washed, sat down to supper, and then praised
The Father whose great mystery remains
This uttered earth His Word alone sustains.

Baked ham from pigs made fat on homegrown grain,
Plates piled with turnips, field peas, lima beans,
Mashed potatoes with red-eye gravy pools,
Cornbread to sop pot licker from the greens,
That was the common fare we relished best,
And after, while the kitchen's built-up heat
Moved out into the early evening cool,
We settled on the porch and put in words
The customary wonders of the day,
Those stories children gathered in their hearts
To blaze in recollection like a faith.
And when at last we had no more to say
We watched the stars whose tale was like our own—
Old yeomen of the cold blue fields of space!—
And knew that deepest peace a freehold brings
Where all is seen and done as sacral act
As on those nights when we could faintly hear
Dry cisterns hiss with warm late summer rains,
While in the bed, flesh answering to flesh,
We filled the womb's rich ground with human seed.

And so we lived for years almost the same
As when we cleared the wilderness and found
High pasturelands still grazed by buffalo
And meadows where the startled bobwhites rose
In choral odes composed of their own name.
Then came that blighted time when cotton lords
Drove us into a war to save their slaves,
Men just like us, yet who had worked the land,
Not as themselves, but others' property.
And in defeat we, too, were all but slaves
Sold into debt and tenantry and lien
Long after Yankees burned our crops and stole
Not only from the planters on the Red
But us as well who might have called them kin,
Those farm boys from Ohio and Vermont.
Yet worst of all was something that broke free
From shattered chains which held it through the war,
A strange, detached, new terrifying mind
Both bestial and angelic in its pride,
A mind that we saw realized in acts
When loggers cut out all the yellow pine
Leaving stripped hills the rains would wash away,
Or when, in bright savannahs, where the pinks
Spread blushing in the flush of early spring,
Great metal wells made dreadful silhouettes
Like huge black praying mantises that bowed
Each time they turned their wheels and from the ground
Pumped up as holy oil the spoiled remains
Of creatures left for ages undisturbed.

In such a world but few of us still live
As neighboring relations on these farms
Whose graveyards bear the same repeated names
Through generations, stone by native stone,
And yet we stay in witness to a time
Before the long poled wires brought telephones
To tell us quick what might have kept a while,
A time when these as yet unclouded skies

Would darken when we saw the massive flocks—
Passenger pigeons!—casting on the ground
Vast shadows of themselves that haunt the mind
Because we still remember how they died:
The men who came by night with torch and rod
Slaughtering whole rookeries for the meat—
A thousand barrels daily to New York!—
The young left in their nests to cry and starve
Until the last bird perished in a zoo
That summer when the war to end all wars
Broke out in mad attacks that would not stop
Till mustard gas, machine guns, tanks, and planes
Blackened the trench-scarred farms of Catholic France.

# THE SOUTH

I am afraid of those Great Suns.
—Emily Dickinson, in 1858, to a friend
spending a summer in New Orleans

*for Andrew Lytle (1902–1995)*

Down here great Sherman suns burned up
The sweetest fields our Aprils bring,
Gay daisies blazed with buttercups,
The cavaliers of spring.

Then summer heat's oppressive strokes
Made drunken sons of memory
Raise Dixies under courthouse oaks
To the sober bust of Lee.

Soon Indian summers of the fall
Possessed them as the past was sold:
They swayed when northern plants grew tall
In goldenrod so gold.

Now trembling ironweeds rust and fold
At a touch of winter chill
While round the courthouse, green and old,
The pastoral oaks grow still.

# OAK ALLEY

*for L. P. S.*

## 1

Having toured the house, old wood restored with care,
You walked the long green corridors of shade
Formed by those great oaks and drew out of the air
A history of the South your musings made.

Your mind went back three hundred years ago
To when an unknown Frenchman drained the land
Clearing virgin wood of ash and tupelo
Set thick in gumbo clays and river sand.

The modest cypress cottage long since gone,
Its trees, planted as saplings to enhance
A dwelling-place, grew massive on the lawn,
Seedlings of Eden, gigantic in their trance.

Perhaps you saw as well young trunks in their prime
Torched by autumn suns along the carriageway
Where sugar princes danced at harvest time,
Their bourbon glasses tinkling on the tray.

Or else a family dinner: deep blue plates
Of willowware filled from hot tureens,
Then placed by slaves in warmers near the grates,
Gravy ladled out over the pastoral scenes.

But most of all you listened for refrains
Sung by exhausted field hands, cries of the heart,
Burdens of an undersong whose strains
In time would tear their masters' world apart.

And though the planters had a case, a right
To their secession, it cannot be denied

That goods begat goods when slaves cut cane by night,
Black acts of agrarian usury and pride.

Then, after the war, history and fiction,
Chronicling this world as though a single art,
Shared the metaphysical dereliction
Of houses they could enter, not depart.

Such disciplines, you sensed, but touched the mysteries:
What deeper craft could teach you more than these?


2


For years you probed to locate deep disease
In the Old South and New England, twin
Empires of modernity, each one at ease
With its own myth of innocence and sin.

Slave worlds of the cotton field and northern mill—
Both marked the bleak distinctions you refined:
The second fall of man from guilt to will,
The war of the secession of the mind.

Chiron's mythic school within the linden trees,
Platonic noons of stilled Ilissian planes,
Scriptoria, universities—in these
You found a third estate the intellect sustains.

Awareness of being, lost to the absurd
In closures of sophistic church and state—
Serving the realm of letters and the Word
You left those mute dominions to their fate.

Yet from your own domain there would emerge
A gnostic science no common tongues contain
But only coded symbols that diverge
From discourse into the wordless dark arcane.

Searching the twilight skies of Christendom,
Oppressed by melancholy and despair,
A wise man, yet a shepherd, you had come
To wonder if the Star was ever there.

Still, in all you wrote, you kept alive old norms—
Edited, annotated, codified—
Made essays that attained primary forms,
And mourned the prose renascence while it died.

Then, like Socrates, hearkening to the end,
You turned to poetry and lately sensed
In Tate and his successors some firm trend
Toward what your musing daimon had evinced:

A southern poetic, Thomistic, undeprived,
Apollo lost in Christ and glorified.


3


These things all held within, you came to stand
Beneath Augustan oaks—dense as the screen
Of history, remote yet close at hand—
And gazed upon the primal southern scene.

Here exiles lost to innocence betrayed
Two rooted peoples, black and native red,
And while the fields of paradise still paid
Heard none but the soothing words their serpent said.

And so, where the Mississippi's foaming mouth
Enters a sunlit gulf and voids its silt,
Rich earth brought forth the Matter of the South
Out of the seeds of chivalry and guilt.

That was the precious blessing: to be cursed
By Eve's plantations, green dreams of Adam's fall,

And thus made proof against the very worst,
A world that cannot taste its bitter gall.

Built in that place by artisans and slaves,
Oak Alley was abandoned, then restored,
Its servants and their masters safe in graves,
Untroubled by the raised or broken sword.

And there like one who versed and harmonized
Apollo's hymn and Aesop, in his cell—
Pure intellect and nature moralized—
You measured out a pastoral citadel

Far from those prose myths of Tara and Legree
Until at last poiesis set you free.

# For John Finlay (1941–1991)

I met you on Good Friday at the wedding
Of a friend, and struck by your strong voice, broad
Forehead, wiry build, and penetrating mind
Determined to know you better.
                                                    Later,
In Baton Rouge, we read each other's poems
Testing the rhythms, images, and rhymes,
Struggling to master this greatest of all crafts,
Craving the grace of one perfected page.
Truly a man of letters who could love
Blunt Johnson and the nuances of James
And ask how that which says "the mind is weak"
Can state its law and yet transcend the same,
You wrote clean abstract poems in plainest style
And sensuous descriptions charged with thought,
Probing toward the source and end of intellect
That marks our place in all the Maker wrought.
Both natives of the South trying to reclaim
Something of Greece and Christendom, we'd walk
To the Union from our desks in Allen Hall
Talking of Homer, Dante, Winters, Tate,
A "Stanford" or a "Simpson" *Southern Review,*
Finding ourselves as poets and as friends
There, at LSU, in those sweet-olive days,
Summer seeming endless in sunlit colonnades.

# AT FRANKLIN

And where, O Allen Tate, are the dead?
—Donald Davidson to Tate, 15 February 1927

*for Charles C. Clark*

1

The dead lie here beneath each measured stone
Anonymous yet known to Him alone
Who holds their souls while undecayed remains
Of dust and bone still touched by winter rains
Sink slowly to a buckled limestone bed
Whose sea had been a word the Maker said.
And opening the gate in autumn light
We come at dusk to know them as we might,
No Eleatic strangers made absurd
By loss of faith in action or the Word,
Nor elegizing hierophants who claim
To keep alive a waning sacred flame
But seekers who would bring to what they find
A loving objectivity of mind.
Such love would tell in time the dead had fought
Not only for the world the planters wrought
But for the sheer adventure, the élan
Of mortal battle called up by blood and clan,
States' rights, escape from boredom on the farm,
Concern that their own kin might come to harm
And at the last perhaps from some vague dread
That *things themselves*, as Davidson once said,
Were being rooted out from given ground,
Then floated in a pool the psyche found
Within itself, mere images displaced
From that full life with which they had been graced.
And thus the nearly fifteen hundred souls
Whose names would soon be stricken from the rolls

Had come to Winstead Hill where state by state
In closing ranks grown still as day grew late
Filled with the grim presentiment of loss
They saw that open ground they had to cross
Confronting Union guns and musketry.
And of these men the men of Tennessee
Alone could gaze again on what they craved,
A land four hundred battles had not saved
Yet held in memory's blood grown flush with love:
Uplands and plateaus once so clouded above
By migrant flocks of pigeons that the sun
Hid by the flapping blackness seemed undone,
Deep rivers and the mountain streams so clear
Running through woods where Indians would spear
The cornered bear or chase a white-tailed doe
In auric glades whose noon's archaic glow
Had lured those first explorers toward a ground
Of open gold the old long hunters found
When one loud shot flushed out a thousand quail
And brought the settlers down the narrow trail
With tools made by and for the human hand
Tempering wilderness to useful land,
This place of common riches—collard greens,
Glazed hams and buttered cornpone, young snap beans
And winesap apples, thick biscuits and the sweet
Spring water welling up, and bourbon neat.
Such memories, once theirs, we hold alone
Inside this fence, spiked iron guarding stone
Where leaves fall as they will and lichens spread
While high in the fluted cedars overhead
Winds carry the last male crickets' rising cries
Toward Franklin as the autumn twilight dies.


2


Hood stood on Winstead Hill as best he might
With crutch and stump, determined on a fight,

His field glasses trained, oblique to failing day
On Franklin where a Union army lay
Dug in on chosen ground it swore to keep
Waiting behind high breastworks and those deep
Empty ditches near which the cannon massed
Against the dream that held him to the last—
To Nashville! turning Sherman from the sea,
Then through the Gap to Grant, crushing him with Lee.
Such was the deadly rhetoric that Hood
Would see enfleshed in bodies dripping blood,
Hyperbole made lethal by a mind's
Wild Viking will that nothing ever binds
To truth but tragic acts beyond control,
Some Celtic fatalism of the soul.
And thus with no artillery, reserves,
Or plan but the dreaded gesture that serves
No further purpose—a charge doomed to halt
At earthworks over fields the blood-drops salt—
Hood ordered the attack as hazy light
Windless and warm gave way to early night,
And soon two corps of eighteen thousand men
Raised up with ragged battle-flags a din
Of hellish yells moving north again,
Gray and butternut over the bluegrass plain.
Ahead, in the coming dusk, rabbits and quail
Panicked as the yells became a wail
When Union guns tore Brown and Cleburne's lines
Mangling legs and torsos, snapping spines
With canister and ball in enfilade
While to the front behind each palisade
Riflemen poured forth concentrated fire
Riddling shattered ranks that staggered in a mire
Of their own guts and blood when the volleys told,
Whole men dissolved in gore no hands could hold.
The works were breached, then sealed, the battle lost
But not yet ended: night brought holocaust.
For pinned beneath huge headlogs by the bank
Of parapets men killed and died point-blank

In those blood-pits of sacrifice so steep
That in the end the dead lay seven deep.
By moonlight, rats and looters roamed at large,
Feasting on the carnage of the charge
While Schofield, as he planned, just slipped away
Leaving the consequences of the day
To one whom smoke and distance and the dark
So blinded that he could not watch the stark
Horror he caused or see how many died,
Including those four generals side by side
Laid out on Carnton's gallery while Hood
Moved on to Nashville, as he swore he would.
And there when ice froze light itself to ground
He saw an iron Zion ringed around
With batteries and breastworks to defend
Its powdermills and foundries without end,
A fortress of numbers, sheer matériel
From which, when pressed, the Rebels fled pell-mell
Their bare split feet streaking snow with blood;
By Forrest screened, they sang of John Bell Hood.


3


The army straggled back through Franklin where the dead
Lay mangled still in trenches while instead
Of marble slabs or tombstones with a name,
Each birth date, and the one death date the same
Which nearly eighteen hundred men now bore,
30 November 1864
Only a few small crosses in the snow
Marked where the frozen bodies thawed below.
Then, in the second spring, McGavock gave
A portion of his land for one great grave
Where state by state beneath each measured stone
The dead remain, anonymous and known.
Yet have we done them justice by the claim
That some "immoderate past" or conjured name—

"Stonewall, Stonewall," "Antietam, Malvern Hill"—
Damns us to inaction, paralyzes will,
Leaving us not wise Clio or the still
Visage of Mnemosyne but a fool
Jaguar leaping to his image in a pool
Or else a sidling Eliotic crab
Washed in a tidal life surely too drab
For any landed man—or by those cries
So partisan, yells rattling into sighs,
Old longings wandering solemnly at large,
"The Army of Tennessee knows how to charge"
(But to what end and under what command
And to defend what cause, to take what stand?),
Or wishing just to say as Cleburne then
"If we are to die, let us die like men"—
Or should we try to voice and usher in
Those truths which history's dead keep hidden still
From that twin face of fixed hermetic will
Whose gazes neither hold nor yet dismiss us:
Nostalgia and Narcissus as Narcissus?
For all the world is Nashville or would be
As seen by Hood before he had to flee
Like him whose deathless mother once revealed
What battle-smoke and matter had concealed,
"Dread shapes come into view—mighty powers"
Whose timeless minds decreed Troy's final hours,
"The gods, the relentless gods" behind the fire:
Neptune, Juno, Pallas, and The Sire.
Yet here, where Hood was blinded by the smoke
And solipsistic will, no goddess spoke,
Nor did the long campaign take us to Rome
But on to Appomattox, Durham, home,
Home to become a self-made bonded race
Compelled to build New Corinth deep in Thrace
And then to come to like it, just as these
Commuters through the twilight's last degrees,
Back now from Nashville, take to a tennis court
Beside the graves where catgut makes report

The ball pocking as the players charge the net
Trading shots in darkness through the set,
Taut muscles moving to a full steady breath,
Their dream the modern dream—to ace out death
Or take him strong with each deep lob and volley
To the final breakpoint—madness and folly
Spared the Mound-Builders whose village once was here,
These dead as well whose stillness draws us near.

# PALM SUNDAY, 1865

*for Shirley*

Stirred ashes of the last encampment glowed
A moment in the dawn that Lenten day
After the night's bleak council had resolved
To try once more to break out to the west
And Lee took to his tent to wait and pray.
The spiked palmettos shivered on the verge
Of Holy Week when Lincoln like a god
Would move through Richmond hailed by faithful slaves
As their redeemer-king, no more than days
From comedy a plot turned passion play.
But as for us who tested federal lines
That Sabbath morning—pressing horse and gun
Until they melted back through those massed corps
Not even Stonewall, God's quick justicer,
Could then have turned and routed, had he lived—
We knew capitulation would confirm
Only what martial force and partial truths
Rooted in new taboos could realize.
And so, though all was lost, those four seared years
Became a demarcation scorched with fire
On breasts possessed by undivided love,
And our defeat just pickets driven in
Along a single front that since has spread
Across the earth in open total war
Gone far beyond the vaunted holocausts
Of Fredericksburg, Cold Harbor, Pickett's Charge.
And though we could not know it at the time
When Traveller passed between the still blue lines—
Surrendered Lee, immaculate in pain—
We sensed that Appomattox made no end
Of this sustained engagement to the death
Between the given world and wild desire.
And that is why Palm Sunday in a Lent

Extending past the fiery pride of those
Whose homes, now ash, had thrown their columned flames
High in the ancient houses of the night,
We rode beyond the lines that Gordon held,
And once more to affirm what we would be,
As truce flags fluttered white by our struck tents
And cherry blossoms fell like April snow,
Across the burning ground of our own lives
We turned and headed south with Fitzhugh Lee.

# THOREAU'S FAREWELL TO CONCORD:
## A MIRROR FOR MODERN MAGISTRATES

*Richard Weaver, i.m.,*
*and for David Bovenizer,*
*who once read Weaver by Walden Pond*


Now that my shoes are mended, once again
I'll shake the dust of Concord from my feet
And follow whims that flutter from within
Leading my heart to drum its rebel beat.

I never joined the family, church, or state
And feel no guilt for duties left undone,
Though who but I was fit to consecrate
Myself as priest and regent of the One?

The pencil factory, Harvard, and the school
Are bodies of no consequence to me.
They served my higher purpose, each a tool
I used to forge a soul in secrecy.

How well I know the fate of Socrates!
Why should I stay to drink such poison down
Administered by those it did not please
To recognize in me a one-man town?

In truth, my night in jail was little more
Than time to eat and sleep and sense again
How right it is to publicly deplore
Each thing my private conscience deems a sin.

I'm glad, of course, my college had its books,
My pupils their tuition, and the Sage
Of Concord work for one on whom he looks
As friend and fellow prophet of the age.

And, yes, I'll wander far in mended shoes
Beyond the cobbler's hammer and his bill,
But that's all past: I'll pay no other dues
Except to follow fancy where it will.

And now some people wait impatiently
For me to lead them up a hill I know
On which there's no authority but me
To show them where God's huckleberries grow.

# The Old Bank in Saline

For what shall it profit a man,
if he should gain the whole world,
and lose his own soul?


The locked front door holds firm though broken panes
Above the worn brass knob go unrepaired.
Late afternoons the tellers' rusted trays
Take in the gold the sun deposits there
Descending through a haze of yellow dust
That settles far beyond all human care.
Beside a filing cabinet's empty drawers
A calendar for 1959
Cut from a southern almanac declares
A January holiday for Lee,
The weather and the moons, best planting times,
Aquarius and Christ's Epiphany.
And through the wavy blocks of jagged glass,
Peering with thick-lensed eyes made dim with age
I'm swept by love's great elegiac sway
Back forty years when I would toddle down
Past open doors and tellers to your lap,
Grandfather Sudduth, president and mayor
Of this small bank and sandy pine hill town.

And even now I seem to find you there
In plain white shirt, black coat, and straight black tie
Leaning over a ledger's columned page,
Your fountain pen dipped deep in purple ink
To reconcile and balance, rectify.
And when you read the numbers and the names
By signatures on mortgages and loans
You did not think of profits maximized
Through sharpness or severity but those
With whom you sat each Sunday as you prayed
Taking to heart the Baptist pastor's fire,

His bony finger tapping at the texts
About the widow's mite and Caesar's things,
Joseph enrolled, the tithe, a Wise Man's gold,
The temple's moneylenders, talents hid,
Or Judas' palm where silver burns the soul.

Thus humbled by God's justice and His love
And led by mercy's prudence you would try
To help indebted neighbors keep their homes,
Building up true community and trust
With honesty from that part mythic time
When handshakes were as good as papers signed.
The girls your loans would send to Normal School,
Come back to teach the farm boys thirty years,
Those boys' own fathers you would let hang on
When mortgage payments fell months in arrears,
Widows whose pension funds were placed so well
They'd all have gladly wed you if they could—
Such private happiness and public good
Defined a world you bettered on the way
Toward modest earnings hard and fairly gained.
And so, unchanged, your probity and word
Sustained you through not only those grave days
When FDR himself would have to write
To shut a bank untouched by panic-runs
But through Ike's richer '50s when you died
Leaving nine thousand dollars and a name
To those the name alone had satisfied.

And now as dying sunlight turns to gold
Those rooms that only memory can restore
To one who knows as you had known before
From what great depths the heart can overflow,
I walk back down to my blue Regal parked
Beside the modern bank that's since replaced
Those old gray walls condemned to slow decay
And see through windows silvered in the dusk
Two young bank officers still working late,

Granddaughters of a man whose land you saved,
Now helping as they once were helped themselves.

And on a wall there hangs a photograph,
A gift I sent in 1994
To celebrate the founding of the bank,
Your image caught some forty years before
In honor of the first half century.
You stand erect in sober, formal pose,
Grandmother Mary Emma at your desk
Beside cut roses floating in their bowls,
Your firm hand on her shoulder gently pressed,
A patriarchal gesture, dated now,
Yet here the source of her contentedness.
Behind you two large pictures fill a shelf,
Grown children missed: Joe Lynn, a country boy
Scarred by fifty missions over the Rhine
Whose bombing left a time bomb in the heart
Exploding in his sleep at forty-five;
And by him in a golden oval frame
Anna Marie, my mother, who lives on
According to her girlhood's social code,
Expecting courtesy, good manners, taste,
Eyes saying all a lady has to say.

Long may such faces gaze from that new bank
As spirits witnessing to other days
And may the old bank building not be razed
For parking space or draw the tourists down
Who might have seen Saline in Newman's *Blaze*.
And may those yellowed ledgers in their dust
Remind us like the Bible that you kept
Beside the books to call you to account
How soon you'd have consigned to bankrupt hells
All loan sharks and those '80s S&Ls
By virtues made the coin of your just realm,
Their worth the legal tender of your ways.

# Hurricane

All summer off West Africa the sun
Poured heat upon the surface of the sea
While coming from the jungle humid winds
Wove up my torrid torso as it spun.
By August I was headed for the South
Following routes the slave ships used to take
Until my spiral bands, great arms of rain,
Would lash across the waste of salt and foam
So I, the dreaded reveler of the waves,
Whose black locks raveled in the stratosphere,
Might dance my dance of death before the Keys
And in the upper Gulf when I broke clear.
And as my eye revolved, huge water-walls
Would trap tired egrets, frigate-birds, and gulls
Flown to the clouded center of my heart
Where swept in the drenched winds swirling around
They drowned aloft, then sank in Breton Sound.
At last I wobbled and stalled along the coast
Where the mouthing Mississippi's lips of silt
Curled as I drove the fecund waters from his bed
Slicing the barrier isles as I would blow
Through twisted willow, oak, and indigo.
Once over land, now holding you in throes,
I spread my fatal waves through salted grass,
Flattened the cane so sweet and green and high,
Tore wires that brought you cooling and the light,
Smashed the chapel spire, plowed up the buried dead,
And left your babies hanging in the trees.
Then feeling weak and mortal from the rage
Of such great dissipation, I drifted east
Breaking up somewhere just north of Boston.
And though again in that strange way you gave
Thanks to your Father-God for being saved,
Accepting devastation as a part
Of that inscrutable act you call the Fall,

Your weathermen are wrong to take away
From half of me those female names so real
For I am Audrey, Betsy, and Camille,
So cast aside that patriarchal myth
And worship me whose pattern is the pith
Of all that is, the brutal womb of things,
Closed systems of the woven dynamos,
And know me as the one who comes and goes,
A fury in the matter I have riven,
Myself the only giver and the given.

# HYACINTH SONG

*for Leslie Alexius*

From mother earth I came to you a gift,
An ornamental beauty rarely seen,
In lily pools and fish ponds set adrift
Where Buddhas smiled belichened and serene.

Once powdered by my pollen I soon grew
By flower and offshoot root till I became
A blossomed god flourishing as I slew
All things I could entangle in my name.

Then pulling me up and flinging me aside
In sewers or in streams you thought to be
Rid of a plant whose beauty you decried
The moment I defied you and broke free.

Spread wide by waterbirds and hurricanes
Who took my seed aloft on wind and wing—
Those lethal storms, great egrets, twisters, cranes—
I throve on death itself, my vital sting.

And blooming on from April until frost,
Changing my size and color as I will,
Choking your waterways forever lost,
I was the virulent mere that none could kill.

Your dynamite and arsenic and fire
Did nothing but disperse me more and more,
My yellow eyes made wider by desire,
My streaming leaves grown green from shore to shore

For beauty, sex, and death are Gaean powers
Aroused by the wheeling aegis of the sun,
These lavender and blue and purple flowers
Divided and dividing from the One.

# THE DUCK HUNT

Male and female created He them. . . .
—Genesis 1:27

*for William Bedford Clark*


Its ricefields bared beneath a hunter's moon,
For miles we crossed an almost treeless plain
South to the shifting edges of the Gulf.
Here doming beds of salt and crumbled marl
Had yielded to the diggers printed stone—
The primal forms of whale and mastodon,
Wide thigh-bones of a woman, shoulders of a man—
Such lay beneath a road of shell and clay
That took us into the marshes where we felt
Our senses heighten and found ourselves again
As hunters and providers, human males.

Black coffee for breakfast, boots pulled up snug
To the hips, in faintest dawn we started out
Driving beside scrub willow to the spot
From which, through silverling, elder, rattlebox,
And matted stands of man-tall yellow sedge,
Pushing out into the shallows we paddled
A light canoe, bearing by the stakes
That marked the cuts between us and our pond.
And there, knee-deep in reed-blinds, camouflaged,
We called to migrant flocks that passed above
This open wilderness of grass and mud.

By night and day, oblivious of time,
Offshore, distant rigs, ringed with warning lights,
Sent down huge bits to breach the ancient layers
And flush up oil a thousand ages made
Consumed in one short century of waste.
But here a saner pace of heartbeat and breath

Returned us to a place we once had held
In fealty to a shared apparent world
Of beast and plant, of mineral and star,
Things trusted to our knowledge, use, and care
Within the givenness of what we are.

Called back from such high musings by the cries
Of canvasbacks and mallards flapping down
To the water, we stood up, aimed, turning
As they wheeled away, firing just ahead
Of each stunned duck that arcing in dead drop
Floated in feathered wreckage on the pond.
Fair marksmen who reached our limit in the dawn,
We loaded the canoe, paddled back to shore,
Slung the chain of birds into the trunk,
And filled with a quiet archaic elation
Passed down from all our fathers, headed home.

# BLUE HERONS

*for Carolyn*

The morning sun inclines us toward its light
Spreading above scrub willow and the sedge
Where swamp gives way at last to marshy ponds
Of pickerel, fire flag, and arrowhead.
And there in mangle-brush and roseau cane,
Black mangrove, matted bullrush, and the dense
Old water-groves of tupelo and gum
Or high within the doming cypress stands
We see the great blue herons in their nests,
Each platform with its clutch of pale green eggs.

Hatched out in June with softest natal down,
The birds become tall stalkers in their prime
Deliberate in movement through the pools
Darting at minnows, frogs, and dragonflies.
Their colonies remain throughout the year
Though when their northern kin who breed in cold
Then gaze toward polar wastes of ice and snow
Are drawn back south by some still hidden sign
Our residents call out while they return
Alighting on the islands and the coast.

We make no noise yet when we start to go
The herons cry and climb as toward a home
On columned drafts between the Gulf and sun,
Alive in fiery light above the foam.
Bright heirs of an almost winterless domain,
They hear our voices rising as they glide
Higher in time's elation and declare
That time is but a flyway to the side
Of one who calls all creatures by their names,
His timbre their intention on the course.

# Beyond the Chandeleurs

> islands reached and named by Iberville,
> 2 February 1699

Old channels of the river's sunken bed
Gone under shores black waters wash and tar
Ten thousand years have swung from side to side
For more than fifty miles through swamp and marsh.
And underneath the waves of Breton Sound
A buried delta settles on the shelf
Worn down by storms and tides nine centuries
Here, where the Mississippi found the Gulf
While Saint Bernard, for whom the place is named,
Inside remote Clairvaux, as tapers blazed,
Praised Mary as the mother of the child
Whose mortal flesh was hers and hers his grace.

And now, three hundred years from Iberville,
This frigid winter dawn the very day
Whose name he gave those shores toward which we sail,
We cross the sound to find the Chandeleurs
So luminous in moonlight, crescent dunes,
Bleak beaches without islands, miles from land,
Forever washed by waves that crash across
Their narrow breadth, channeling in the sand.
And as we pass by slowly, south-southwest,
We see in mingled gleams of moon and sun
Bubbling over the salt in windblown foam
The play of shape and chaos, our true home.

So, too, as that grim interim—the Break—
Rent Christendom in 1699
Iberville sailed on, blind through sleet and fog,
Threading the low marsh islands, mud-drift logs,
And those hooked spits of swirling sea and earth,
Moving through uncreation where his men
Would dig deep pits to make freshwater wells

And sleep on planks above the flooding strand.
Yet when at last he reached the Chandeleurs,
Whose myrtles yielded wax for Candlemas,
He tasted in the wind-borne glazing rain
Sweet water from the Mississippi's mouth.

And though we find no myrtles on these shores
We still can glimpse within each twinkling grain,
So near black dregs of marshes and the rigs,
Glimmering hints old Simeon discerned
In eyes that glowed with heaven's native light
Just as the stars, like whorling hurricanes,
Come from the vast galactic nursing-grounds,
Candles that burn in scattered grains of flame,
Now blaze the blatant purpose of the world
Beyond the Chandeleurs that still remain
Within this star-torched temple love preserves
Declaring till the end their given name.